Adventures in Pet Sitting

Happy House

About Wise & Wide

- A systematic 6-level English reading program based on Lexile® measures
- Diverse and interesting topics chosen from the elementary curriculums of Korea and English speaking western countries
- Well-written books in various forms including fiction stories, descriptive texts, and classics retold
- The informative but original fiction stories grab your interest, leading to the easy and clear understanding of the educational content.
- Improve thinking skills with solid after-reading activities at all levels of the series.

Wise & Wide is a 6-level English reading program that consists of 60 books and each level is systematically divided by Lexile® measures. The Lexile® Framework for Reading is the most popular reading measuring system in American formal education curriculums and many English programs. Over 20 out of 50 states in the U.S. mark Lexile® measures directly on students' final report cards and over 300 well-known publishers adopt and use Lexile® measures.

Experience many kinds of readings written by professional writers from the U.S. and England. They used interesting topics that were carefully chosen after analyzing elementary curriculums from around the world including Korea, the U.S., England, and Australia among many others. Comprehensive after-reading activities including graphic organizers, speaking tasks, and After-reading Tests are ready for you.

Levels in the series and their corresponding Lexile® measures

Level	Lexile® measures	U.S. Grade
Level 1	Below 200L	Pre K - K
Level 2	190L - 400L	Lower Grade 1
Level 3	350L - 530L	Upper Grade 1
Level 4	420L - 650L	Grade 2
Level 5	520L - 940L	Grade 3 - 4
Level 6	830L - 1070L	Grade 5 - 6

* Smart Readers: Wise & Wide level 1 is applicable to the preschool level in the U.S.
* The source of the relationship between Lexile® measures and U.S. school grades: CCSS(Common Core State Standards) FOR ENGLISH LANGUAGE ARTS, APPENDIX A (2012, which is used by 45 states in the U.S.)

Topic List

	Level 1	Level 2	Level 3	Level 4	Level 5	Level 6
Book 1	Science>Biology: The hibernation of animals Story	Science>Biology: Living and nonliving things Story	Science>Biology> Animals & the Environment: Sea otters Story	Environment> Living with nature: The diver & the persimmon tree Story	Science>Biology> Animal: Amazing animals of the Amazon Story	Science>Biology: Germs, transmitted diseases Story
Book 2	Literature> World classics: Aesop's fables Story	Literature> Traditional fairy tale: Old tales about stones Story	Social Studies> Economy: To run a business to make and save money Story	Science>Biology> Plants: Photosynthesis Story	Science>Earth science: Earth's layers,earthquakes, volcanoes, and earth's atmosphere Report	Mathematics> Sequence: The golden ratio & the Fibonacci sequence Story
Book 3	Science>Physics: How shadows are formed Story	Literature> World classics: Peter Pan Story	Science>Scientific technology: Nanobots Story	Literature>Myths: World's creation stories Story	Literature> Legend: The story of King Arthur Story	
Book 4	Literature> Traditional literature: The Talmud Story	Science>Biology> Animal: Polar bears Story	Science>Biology> Animal: Mountain gorillas Story	Social Studies> Cultural anthropology: Amazing ancient cultures of the world Story	Science> Earth science: Clouds and weather Story	
Book 5			Social Studies> Cultural anthropology: Astonishing festivals Report	Art>Music: Stories from two operas Story		
Book 6				Social Studies> People: Three great people who overcame hardships Story		
Book 7						
Book 8						
Book 9						
Book 10						

* 10 books in each level will be published.

How to Use This Book

•Before Reading

You can easily find the topic and what kind of story you are about to read.

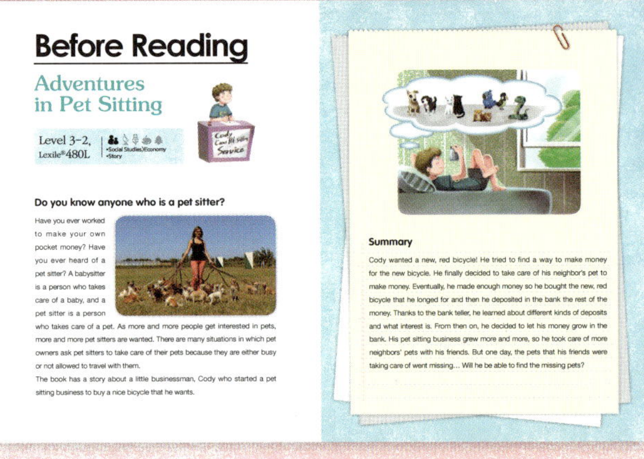

•The text

All the stories were written by professional writers from the U.S. and England, so you will read authentic and appropriate English sentences and expressions in every book in the series.

•Pop Quiz

Check out right away if you understand what you have just read by solving a pop quiz that checks your comprehension.

•Key Words

The key words and expressions on each page are listed for you to easily study them.

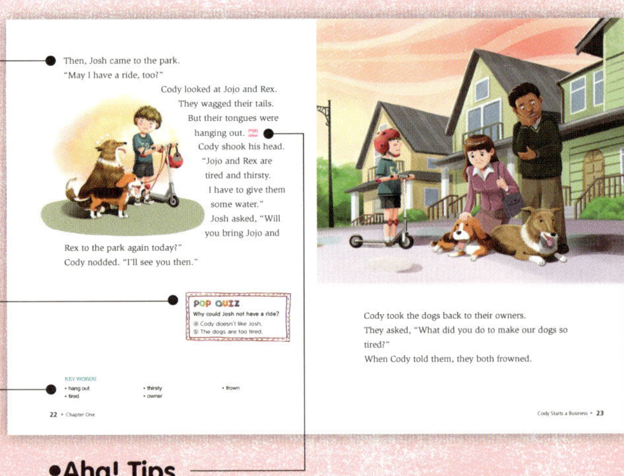

•Aha! Tips

Download free Korean explanations at *www.ihappyhouse.co.kr* for all of the sentences marked with "Aha!". These explain cultural, scientific, and economic knowledge or they deal with aspects of English such as grammatical structures or idiomatic expressions. There are lots of "Aha! Tips" to help you understand the text.

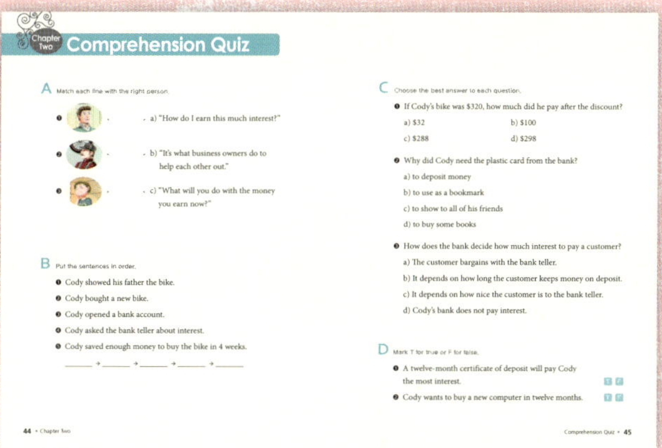

•Comprehension Quiz

After reading one chapter, solve various questions to find out if you fully understand the content.

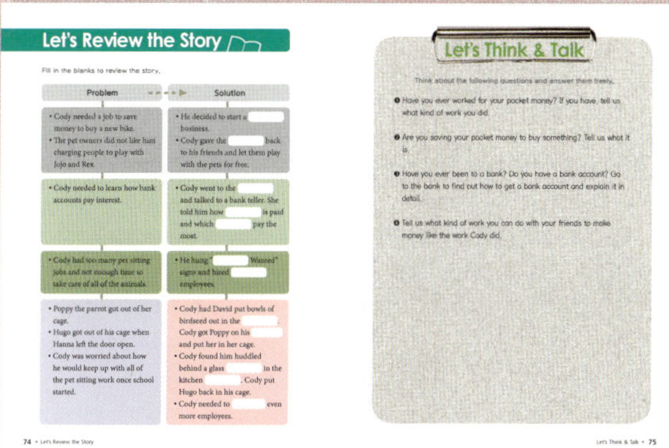

•Let's Review the Story /
•Let's Think & Talk

Fill in the blanks in the organizer to summarize the whole story. Express your own thinking and feelings about the story by answering the questions. You can build up logic and reasoning skills for your essay examinations in the future.

Appendix

Audio CD

In the CD audio book form, the texts are read vividly by American professional voice actors.

After-reading Test

Solve an additionally provided After-reading Test for each book.

The Korean translation, Answer Keys, a Word Quiz, a Word List, and Aha! Tips for each book

You can download them for free at *www.ihappyhouse.co.kr*

Before Reading

Adventures in Pet Sitting

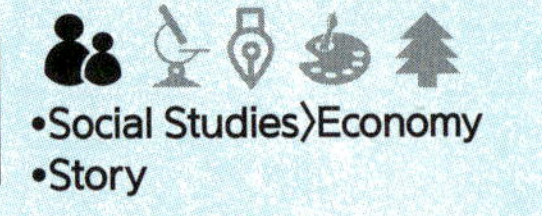

Level 3-2,
Lexile® 480L

• Social Studies〉Economy
• Story

Do you know anyone who is a pet sitter?

Have you ever worked to make your own pocket money? Have you ever heard of a pet sitter? A babysitter is a person who takes care of a baby, and a pet sitter is a person who takes care of a pet. As more and more people get interested in pets, more and more pet sitters are wanted. There are many situations in which pet owners ask pet sitters to take care of their pets because they are either busy or not allowed to travel with them.

The book has a story about a little businessman, Cody who started a pet sitting business to buy a nice bicycle that he wants.

Summary

Cody wanted a new, red bicycle! He tried to find a way to make money for the new bicycle. He finally decided to take care of his neighbor's pet to make money. Eventually, he made enough money so he bought the new, red bicycle that he longed for and then he deposited in the bank the rest of the money. Thanks to the bank teller, he learned about different kinds of deposits and what interest is. From then on, he decided to let his money grow in the bank. His pet sitting business grew more and more, so he took care of more neighbors' pets with his friends. But one day, the pets that his friends were taking care of went missing… Will he be able to find the missing pets?

Adventures in Pet Sitting

Adventures in
Pet Sitting

Chapter One

Cody Starts a Business

Cody wanted a new red bike with fast tires and shiny foot pegs.

"What is wrong with your scooter?" his father asked. **Aha!**

"My scooter is fine. But on a new bike I can go faster."

His father nodded.

"Save your money. Then, you can buy a new bike."

Cody's heart dropped.

He went to his room and looked at his money jar.

▲ scooter

KEY WORDS

- business
- foot pegs
- nod
- save money
- one's heart drops

- jar
- take the lid off (take-took-taken)
- tip
- make money (make-made-made)
- think and think (think-thought-thought)

He took the lid off the jar.

He tipped his money into his hand.

Three silver coins were all he had.

Cody needed a job.

He needed a job to make money for a bike.

What could he do?

Cody thought and thought.

Start a lemonade stand?

Cody decided that was too slow.

Have a car wash?

Cody decided that was too messy.

Mow lawns?

Cody's friend Josh already had a lawn service.

What about pet sitting? **Aha!**

Cody liked animals. Animals liked Cody.

Pet sitting was the perfect business for him.

He got out some heavy paper, colored markers, and clear tape.

Cody made signs for his new business.

They read, "I will help you with your pets.

Call Cody Cares Pet Sitting Service. 555-0132."

KEY WORDS

- lemonade
- stand
- car wash
- messy
- mow lawns

- pet sitting
- perfect
- get out (get-got-gotten)
- marker
- clear

- sign
- read (read-read-read)
- care

The next morning, he hung the signs at the post office and the park.

He hung them at the store and the hair salon.

He hung them at the deli and the doctor's office. 

▲ deli

KEY WORDS

- **hang** (hang-hung-hung)
- **hair salon**
- **doctor's office**
- **walk**
- **pay**

That afternoon, he got his first phone call.

"Cody, will you walk my dog Jojo?

I don't have time when I am working."

Cody said, "I will walk Jojo for twenty minutes in the

morning and twenty minutes in the evening."

"Perfect!"

The woman said she would pay him every week.

Later that day, he got another customer.

This dog's name was Rex.

Cody rode his scooter to pick up Jojo at 8:00 a.m.

Cody tied Jojo's leash to his scooter handlebar.

Jojo pulled Cody to the next house.

"Rex is ready," the man told Cody.

Cody tied Rex's leash to the other handlebar.

Rex and Jojo ran to the park.

They pulled Cody on his scooter all the way.

David saw his friend Cody
with the dogs.
"That looks like fun!"
he said.
"It is fun," Cody
told him.
"The dogs are
having fun, too."
Rex barked.
Jojo barked.
Both dogs wagged
their tails. Aha!
Hanna saw the dogs pulling Cody.
She jumped off the swings and ran to him.

"May I have a ride?"

David asked just as she arrived.

"Me, too!" Hanna said.

"I want a ride with the dogs."

Cody shook his head.

"I don't know. My job is to take care of these dogs."

"We like dogs," David told him.

"We can help take care of them," Hanna said. 

"Please?" they both asked.

"May we have a ride?"

Then, Cody had an idea.

He thought it was a smart idea.

> ## POP QUIZ
>
> **Mark T for true or F for false.**
>
> The children wanted to ride the scooter and let the dogs pull them. T / F

KEY WORDS

- have a ride
- just as
- shake one's head (shake-shook-shaken)
- take care of

Cody could make even more money from his pet sitting service.

"You may have a ride if you pay me one dollar," Cody said.

"I have to go home and get some money."

Hanna ran back to her house.

David reached in his pants pocket.

"Here's one dollar."

He gave it to Cody.

Cody handed the scooter to David.

David got on, and the dogs started running.

David laughed as he rode the scooter.

KEY WORDS

- even
- reach
- hand
- get on
- laugh
- be done
- **bring** (bring-brought-brought)
- take a ride

When he was done, Hanna came back.

She brought her friend Ginny.

Ginny gave Cody one dollar and took a ride.

Hanna gave Cody one dollar and took a ride.

Then, Josh came to the park.

"May I have a ride, too?"

Cody looked at Jojo and Rex.

They wagged their tails.

But their tongues were

hanging out. 

Cody shook his head.

"Jojo and Rex are

tired and thirsty.

I have to give them

some water."

Josh asked, "Will

you bring Jojo and

Rex to the park again today?"

Cody nodded. "I'll see you then."

KEY WORDS

- hang out
- tired
- thirsty
- owner
- frown

Cody took the dogs back to their owners.

They asked, "What did you do to make our dogs so tired?"

When Cody told them, they both frowned.

That night at dinner, Cody's dad said, "Two dog owners called me today."

"What did they say?" Cody asked.

"They said you used their dogs to make money. Plus, they paid you money to walk their dogs."

Cody nodded.

"Yes, sir. But it sounds bad when you say it that way."

"Do you think it's right to make double the money from another person's pet?" his father asked. **Aha!**

Cody thought about it.

"I guess not. From now on, I'll let people ride my scooter for free."

"That's a good idea," his father said.

"You should give the children their money back, too."

KEY WORDS

- plus
- sound
- double
- I guess not.

- from now on
- let (let-let-let)
- for free
- earn

- neighborhood
- behind
- play catch

The next morning, Cody gave Hanna, Ginny, David, and Josh their money back.

But he still had the money he had earned from his pet sitting business.

All of the children in the neighborhood loved it when Cody walked the dogs.

They had fun riding on the scooter behind the dogs.

They had fun playing catch with them.

A Fill in each blank with the right word(s) below.

money   foot pegs   time   one dollar

❶ Cody wanted a bike with fast tires and shiny ______________.

❷ Hanna ran back to her house to get some ______________.

❸ Cody's first customer wanted him to walk her dog because she didn't have ______________ when she was working.

❹ Cody charged his friends ______________ to ride his scooter.

B Mark T for true or F for false.

❶ Cody told the first customer he could walk Jojo for 40 minutes per day.   T F

❷ Cody walked the dogs around the town.   T F

❸ Cody's friend David already had a lawn service.   T F

❹ The children played catch with the dogs in the park.   T F

 Choose the best answer to each question.

❶ Why did Cody decide NOT to have a car wash?

a) He could not get soap and buckets.

b) He did not have enough towels.

c) He did not have a car.

d) He decided that was too messy.

❷ Why did the owners frown when Cody returned their dogs?

a) Cody used their dogs to make more money.

b) Cody did not walk the dogs.

c) Cody returned the dogs very late.

d) The dogs were both muddy.

D Put the sentences in order.

❶ The children gave money to Cody and rode the scooter behind the dogs.

❷ Cody made signs for his new business.

❸ Two dog owners called Cody's dad.

❹ Cody wanted a new bike.

__________ → __________ → __________ → __________

Chapter Two

Biking and Banking

Before long, Cody had many more customers.

He took care of dogs and cats.

He took care of hamsters and birds.

He even took care of a pet snake.

He had to get up early every morning to take care of the pets. **Aha!**

He had to feed them, give them water, clean their cages, and play with them.

POP QUIZ

Fill in the blanks.

To take care of the pets, Cody had to give them _________ and clean their _________.

KEY WORDS

- **before long**
- **feed** (feed-fed-fed)
- **cage**

All of those pets gave Cody good exercise, and he had fun taking care of them.

He earned money for every pet he took care of.

He saved his money every week.

In four weeks, he saved enough cash in his money jar to buy the red bike!

KEY WORDS

- exercise
- enough
- cash

Cody walked into Beamer's Bike Shop.

Cody proudly said to Mr. Beamer, "I'm ready to buy the red bike in the window."

Mr. Beamer pointed to the bike.

"This one with the custom seat and the shiny foot pegs?"

"That's the one."

KEY WORDS

- into
- proudly
- be ready to
- in the window
- point to
- custom

Cody walked over to it and ran his hand over the handlebar.

Mr. Beamer let out a low whistle.

"This is an expensive bike."

"I saved all of the money to pay for it myself."

Mr. Beamer's eyebrows went up in surprise.

"I've been running my own pet sitting business, and I have lots of clients."

Mr. Beamer shook Cody's hand.

"Let me congratulate you on your successful business and wise money skills.

It's hard work running a business."

"Thank you."

Cody stood up straight and pushed his chest out.

"As a fellow businessman, I'm going to give you a cash discount of 10%." Aha!

Cody's eyes lit up.

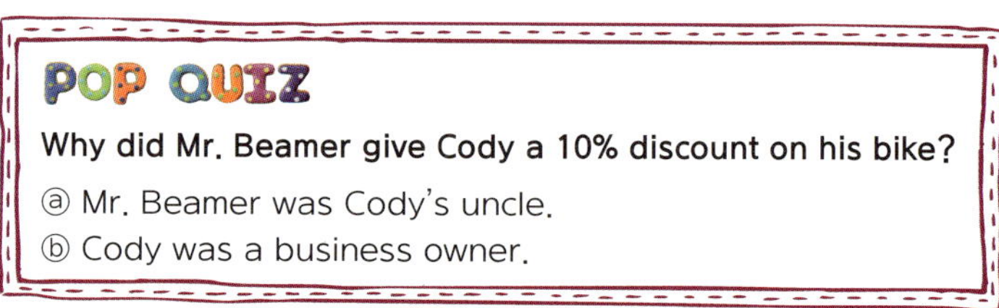

KEY WORDS

- run a business
- client
- shake one's hand
- congratulate
- successful
- wise
- push out
- fellow

- give a discount (give-gave-given)
- light up (light-lit-lit)
- lower
- ring up (ring-rang-rung)
- cash register
- business owner
- help out

- each other
- oil
- remove
- replace
- as much (...) as
- responsibility

"You'll give me a lower price just because I have a business?"

Mr. Beamer rang up the sale on the cash register.

"It's what business owners do to help each other out."

Mr. Beamer showed Cody how to take care of his bike.

He showed him how to oil the chain.

He showed him how to put air in the tires.

He showed him how to remove and replace the foot pegs.

Cody thought taking care of his bike would be almost as much responsibility as taking care of pets.

A few minutes later, Cody strapped on his new helmet and proudly rode home on his sleek new bike.

His father admired the bike.

He nodded his head in approval.

"What will you do with the money you earn now?" his father asked.

"I will save half of my money in the bank," Cody told him.

"That's a wise thing to do. **Aha!**

The bank will pay you money when you make a deposit."

His father looked at his watch.

"The bank is still open now."

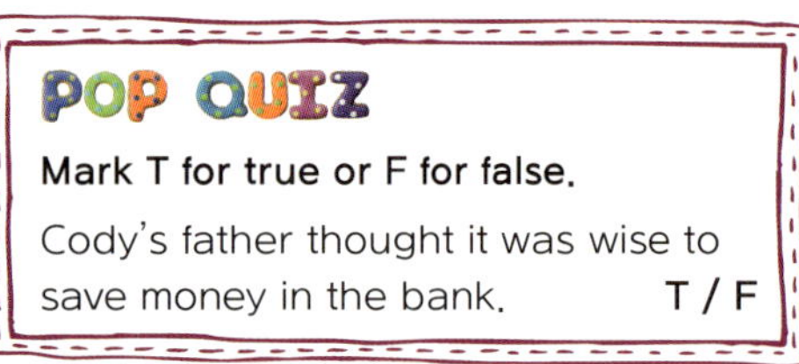

KEY WORDS

- strap
- sleek
- admire
- approval

- half of
- make a deposit
- still

BANK

Cody jumped on his bike and rode it to the bank.

He locked up his bike and went inside.

"How do I open a savings account?"

Cody asked a woman at the counter.

"I'll help you," the bank teller said.

She sat down at her computer and started typing.

"We pay you interest when you put your money in an account," the bank teller told him.

"How does that work?"

Cody looked at all of the signs with percentages on them.

"If you open a savings account, we will pay you this much."

The teller pointed to a small number.

"If you need your money, you can have it.

But if you leave it in the bank, in a few months, you'll have more in your account than if you just save it in your money jar at home."

"That sounds good to me."

"The money we pay you is called interest.

We put it into your account each month."

Cody pointed to a bigger number.

"How do I earn this much interest?"

The teller smiled.

"That is called a CD, or a certificate of deposit. **Aha!**

It says you agree to leave your money in your account

and not use it for twelve months."

"Twelve months is a long time."

"Yes, but if you want to save for something big, you'll

earn twice as much money with a CD.

Your money will grow faster."

Cody thought about the old computer his family used.

Perhaps he could open a CD and save his money to buy

a better computer.

KEY WORDS

- bigger
- certificate of deposit(= CD)
- agree
- twice as much

BILLY
BANK

The teller pointed to an even bigger number.

"This is our college savings account. 

When you put money in this account, you promise to

use it to pay for a university education."

Cody wanted to go to college.

He knew it would be expensive for his family.

"Since you'll be leaving your money here even longer,

we pay you more."

"Sign me up for those accounts, too."

Cody used the money he saved from his cash discount with Mr. Beamer to open a CD and a college savings account.

The teller handed him a plastic card with his account number on it.

"Keep this card. You will use it when you deposit money in your bank accounts."

Cody put the card in a safe place in his wallet.

KEY WORDS

- college savings account
- promise
- university
- education
- since
- sign up
- plastic
- deposit

When he was done, he shook hands with the teller.

He remembered how happy he felt when he bought his
bike earlier that day.

Giving his mother and father a new computer would
make Cody even happier.

Imagine how proud he would feel to graduate from
college while knowing he helped pay for it, too! **Aha!**

Cody was ready to start growing his money in the bank.

He felt like a money wizard!

POP QUIZ

What would make Cody feel happier?

ⓐ to buy a new computer for his parents
ⓑ to make more money with magic

KEY WORDS

- remember
- earlier
- happier
- imagine

- graduate from
- while
- wizard

Comprehension Quiz

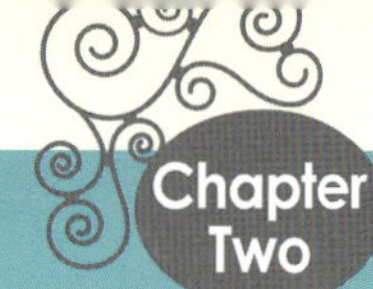

A Match each line with the right person.

❶ •

• a) "How do I earn this much interest?"

❷ •

• b) "It's what business owners do to help each other out."

❸ •

• c) "What will you do with the money you earn now?"

B Put the sentences in order.

❶ Cody showed his father the bike.

❷ Cody bought a new bike.

❸ Cody opened a bank account.

❹ Cody asked the bank teller about interest.

❺ Cody saved enough money to buy the bike in 4 weeks.

______ → ______ → ______ → ______ → ______

 Choose the best answer to each question.

❶ If Cody's bike was $320, how much did he pay after the discount?

a) $32

b) $100

c) $288

d) $298

❷ Why did Cody need the plastic card from the bank?

a) to deposit money

b) to use as a bookmark

c) to show to all of his friends

d) to buy some books

❸ How does the bank decide how much interest to pay a customer?

a) The customer bargains with the bank teller.

b) It depends on how long the customer keeps money on deposit.

c) It depends on how nice the customer is to the bank teller.

d) Cody's bank does not pay interest.

D Mark T for true or F for false.

❶ A twelve-month certificate of deposit will pay Cody the most interest.　　T　F

❷ Cody wants to buy a new computer in twelve months.　　T　F

Chapter Three

Pets on the Loose!

Cody had a problem.

He had too many pets to take

care of and not enough time.

"This is too much work for one person," Cody thought.

"I need to hire someone to help me."

He made more signs.

He used heavy paper, colored markers, and clear tape.

# Cody's Pet Sitting Service

Cody rode on his new red bike all over the neighborhood.

He hung signs at the store and the hair salon.

He hung signs at the deli and the doctor's office.

He hung signs at the post office and the park.

The signs read, "Help wanted. Children preferred.

Call Cody Cares Pet Sitting Service. 555-0132."

KEY WORDS

- on the loose
- problem
- hire
- all over
- Help wanted.
- prefer

That afternoon, he had a line of children in his front yard.

"We want to apply for the pet sitting job," they told him.

Cody asked the children how much experience they had
taking care of pets.

Cody hired Hanna.

She had pets of her own. She even had a horse.

He hired David.

Jojo and Rex liked David best of all the applicants for
the job.

Cody told David and Hanna whose pets they could take care of and at what time. **Aha!**

He wrote it all down on a calendar.

He wrote down how much he would pay his employees for each animal they took care of.

Cody still took care of pets, but now he had to keep track of Hanna's and David's work, too.

Cody's customers paid him every week.

Then, he paid Hanna and David part of the money.

He kept the rest of the money because he owned the business.

POP QUIZ

Why did Cody hire Hanna?

ⓐ Jojo and Rex liked her very much.
ⓑ She had her own pets.

KEY WORDS

- a line of
- front yard
- apply for
- experience
- of one's own
- applicant
- calendar
- employee
- keep track of
- **keep** (keep-kept-kept)

He put half of his money in the bank.

Cody made extra money by having employees.

With employees, he could have more customers.

Now Cody had even more business.

He and his employees took care of tropical fish.

They took care of turtles and lizards. **Aha!**

They even took care of rabbits and a ferret.

Everyone, as well as the pets, was happy.

But one day, a disaster happened.

Cody was at the park with two poodles named Betty and
Bob.

Ring! Ring!

His phone rang.

▲ lizard

- extra
- tropical fish
- turtle
- lizard
- ferret
- as well as
- disaster
- happen
- poodle
- name
- ring

"Cody, it's Hanna.

I'm at Mrs. Taylor's house."

Hanna sounded worried.

"Hugo is missing!"

"You mean Hugo the hamster got out of his cage?" Cody
asked.

"Yes. I went to wash his water bottle, and I forgot to
close the gate on his cage."

Hanna talked fast, and she sounded out of breath.

"I looked everywhere, but I can't find him."

"Did you look in the closet?"

"Yes."

"Did you look under the bed?"

"Yes."

"Did you look under the couch?"

"Yes. I looked in the bathroom and the kitchen, too."

Hanna needed help.

Mrs. Taylor had a fluffy cat with white paws that would love to eat Hugo. **Aha!**

If the cat got hold of Hugo, Cody's business could be ruined.

"I'll be right there," Cody told her.

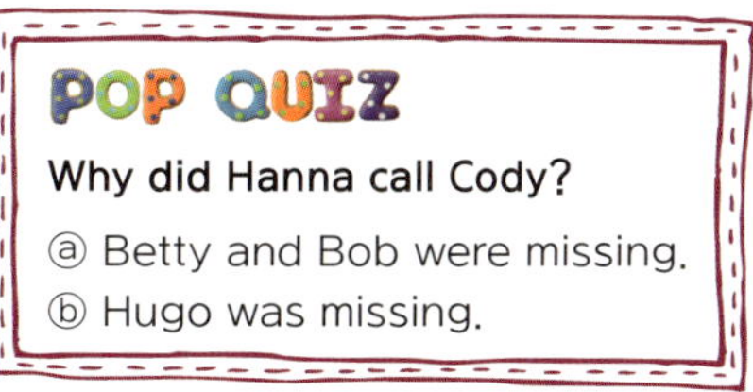

KEY WORDS

- worried
- be missing
- water bottle
- **forget** (forget-forgot-forgotten)

- out of breath
- closet
- couch
- fluffy

- get hold of
- be ruined

He was almost at Mrs. Taylor's house when Cody's phone rang again.

This time it was David.

"Poppy escaped!" David shouted.

"How did Poppy escape?"

Poppy was Mr. King's green parrot.

"I was cleaning her cage, and she flew out the window!"

Cody groaned and rubbed his hand on his face.

"Do you see Poppy now?"

"No, but I hear her squawking," David told him. **Aha!**

At least Poppy hadn't flown away.

Perhaps she was still in a tree near the house.

"I'll be right there," Cody said.

Just then, Josh walked by on the sidewalk.

"Josh, I need your help!"

Cody handed the scooter and the dog leashes to Josh.

"Will you take Betty and Bob for a walk?

I have to help Hanna and David."

"Are you going to charge me a dollar?" Josh was
suspicious.

"No. In fact, I'll pay you a dollar if you take care of Betty
and Bob for me." **Aha!**

"It's a deal!" Josh smiled.

Josh rode the scooter down the block with the dogs.

Cody didn't know where to go first.

Should he go to Mrs. Taylor's house to find Hugo?

If he didn't find Hugo in time, the cat might eat him.

KEY WORDS

- walk by
- sidewalk
- charge
- suspicious
- It's a deal!
- block
- in time
- cabinet
- sink
- hide (hide-hid-hidden)
- space
- lay
- birdseed

Should he go to Mr. King's house to find Poppy?

If he didn't find Poppy in time, she might fly away.

He called Hanna.

"Look in all of the cabinets and under all of the sinks,"
he told her.

"Hamsters like to hide in small spaces."

He called David.

"Lay bowls of birdseed out all over the yard.

When Poppy gets hungry, she will come to eat."

Comprehension Quiz

A Who cares for each of the following animals and what is each animal's name? Match each animal and its name with the right person.

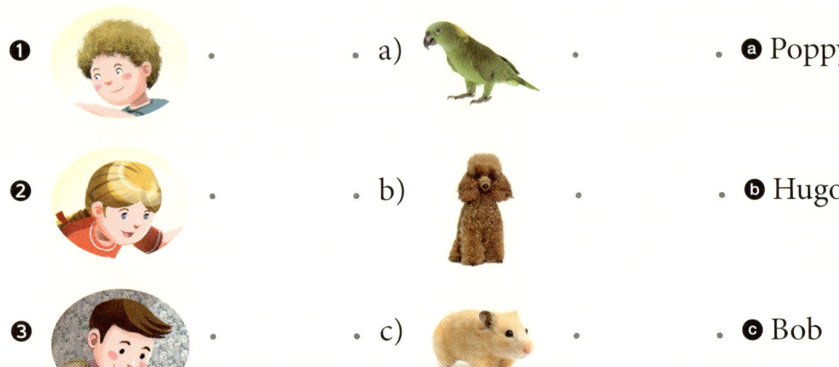

❶   •   • a)   •   • ⓐ Poppy

❷   •   • b)   •   • ⓑ Hugo

❸   •   • c)   •   • ⓒ Bob

B Mark T for true or F for false.

❶ Cody had too many pets to take care of.   T   F

❷ Hanna looked for Hugo in the bedroom and front yard.   T   F

❸ Josh took Betty and Bob for a walk to help Cody.   T   F

❹ Jojo and Rex liked David best of all of the applicants.   T   F

 Choose the best answer to each question.

❶ When Cody was paid each week, what did he do with the money?

a) He spent it.

b) He put $25 in the bank.

c) He put half his money in the bank.

d) He put $50 in the bank.

❷ What was Cody doing when the animals escaped?

a) playing video games

b) watching television

c) jogging at the lake

d) walking Betty and Bob at the park

D Put the sentences in order.

❶ Cody told David to put bowls of birdseed in the yard.

❷ Hanna called Cody and told him Hugo was missing.

❸ Cody asked Josh to take care of Betty and Bob.

❹ David called Cody and told him Poppy was missing.

________ → ________ → ________ → ________

Pet Rescues

When Cody got to Mr. King's house, there was a flock of birds on the lawn.

All of the birds were eating seeds and chirping.

It was a bird party!

"Is Poppy here?" Cody asked David.

David pointed to a bright green and yellow bird.

The bird flew low from one bowl to another.

"Poppy is having too much fun.
She won't come to me." Aha!
Cody gave a soft whistle.
He tiptoed toward Poppy.

KEY WORDS

- flock
- seed
- chirp
- tiptoe

Poppy turned her head and looked at Cody.

He held out a finger for her to climb onto.

Poppy hopped away and ate some more seeds.

Cody whistled again.

Poppy turned her head and looked at him again.

He held out a hand with some seeds in it.

Poppy chirped. She hopped onto his hand.

"Good girl, Poppy!"

Cody whispered to the parrot.

She nibbled at the seeds in his hand.

Cody carried Poppy back to her cage and put her inside.

He quickly shut the door.

Poppy climbed on her perch.

She whistled and talked in her cage.

"That was a close call!"
he told David.

"Now I have to help Hanna
find Hugo."

"You helped me,
so I'll help you,"
David told him.

What did Poppy hop onto?

ⓐ Cody's hand
ⓑ David's arm

KEY WORDS

- **hold out** (hold-held-held)
- **hop**
- **away**
- **whisper**
- **nibble**
- **quickly**
- **perch**
- **a close call**

They raced to Mrs. Taylor's house.

Inside, Hanna was on her hands and knees.

She crawled and looked under all of the chairs and tables.

"Did you look in the cabinets?" Cody asked.

"Most of them," Hanna told him.

"Where is Socks, the cat?" David asked.

Cody, David, and Hanna all looked at each other.

"That's a good question," Hanna said.

"David, check the bathroom cabinets.

I'll look in the kitchen," Cody said.

When Cody went into the kitchen, he found Socks.

Socks sat in front of the sink.

▲ Cats and hamsters are natural enemies.

Socks was staring at the cabinet door.

"What are you looking at?" Cody asked.

"Meow!" Socks answered.

He licked his lips.

Cody picked up Socks and carried him to the living room.

- race
- on one's hands and knees
- crawl
- stare at
- lick one's lips
- pick up

"I think I know where Hugo is," he told Hanna.

"Hold Socks for me."

He went back to the kitchen and opened the cabinet door.

Hugo huddled behind a glass vase.

His nose twitched.

His whiskers quivered.

"Come here, boy," Cody whispered.

He scooped Hugo into his hands.

He put Hugo in his cage with some fresh sawdust and clean water.

He closed the door to the cage and locked it.

Hugo jumped in his hamster wheel and began running.

Then, he curled up for a nap in his cage.

"That was another close call!" Cody said.

KEY WORDS

- huddle
- twitch
- whisker
- quiver
- scoop
- sawdust
- curl up
- for a nap

The three friends went outside.

Josh rode up on the scooter behind Betty and Bob.

"Let's take the dogs home," Cody said.

"Then, let's get some ice cream."

"We made a good team.

We saved all of the pets!" Hanna said.

David laughed.

"You mean Cody saved the pets."

"I could not have done it without your help,"
Cody said.
"You all earned a bonus today.
I will buy the ice cream," he told them.
The four friends shook hands.
"Let's all ride our new bikes to the ice cream shop,"
Hanna said.
"Yes, since we all had jobs this summer, we all saved
money for new bikes!" David said.

They rode to the ice cream shop together.
They all had two scoops of ice cream to celebrate their
pet sitting adventure.

POP QUIZ

What is the bonus Cody is going to give to
his friends?

ⓐ some extra money
ⓑ ice cream

KEY WORDS

- make a good team
- bonus
- celebrate

Cody felt proud. He had started a new business.

He had helped his friends get jobs and save money.

Now they all had new bikes and money in the bank.

But Cody had a problem.

"What will we do when school starts?" he asked his friends.

"We won't have time to take care of all of the pets."

"You can hire more employees to take care of the pets," said David.

"That's right," Hanna said.

"You can hire more children to work before and after school."

Cody nodded.

"That's a good idea.

But there's one more thing I need to do."

"What's that?" the children asked.

"I'm going to need a bigger calendar," Cody said.

They all laughed and finished eating their ice cream.

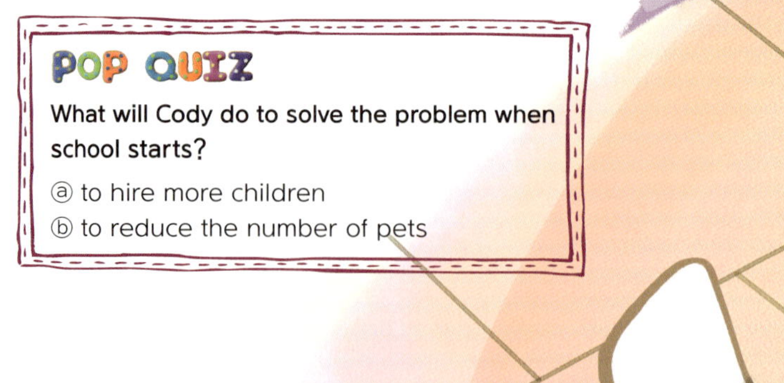

POP QUIZ

What will Cody do to solve the problem when school starts?

ⓐ to hire more children
ⓑ to reduce the number of pets

Sunday Monday Tuesday Wednesday Thursday Friday Saturday
1 2 3 4 5 6
7 8 9 10 11 12 13
14 15 16 17 18 19 20
21 22 23 24 25 26 27

Comprehension Quiz

A Fill in each blank with the right word(s) below.

> whistled　　ice cream shop　　proud　　nap

❶ Poppy looked at Cody when he _______________.

❷ Hugo curled up for a _______________ after he ran in his hamster wheel.

❸ Cody felt _______________ because he had started a new business.

❹ After rescuing the pets, the children rode their bikes to the _______________.

B Mark T for true or F for false.

❶ Poppy was having fun with the other birds.　　T　F

❷ Hanna was on her hands and knees at Mr. King's house.　　T　F

❸ Cody found Socks in front of the cabinet in the bathroom.　　T　F

❹ Cody would not have enough time to take care of all of the pets when school stared.　　T　F

 Choose the best answer to each question.

❶ Why did Poppy finally hop onto Cody's hand?

a) She liked his whistling.

b) She wanted the seeds in Cody's hand.

c) She was tired and wanted to go inside.

d) He offered her a new toy.

❷ Why were the children worried about where Socks the cat was?

a) Socks was the owner's favorite cat.

b) Socks needed to go to the vet.

c) Socks might want to eat Hugo.

d) Socks had scratched the furniture.

D Put the sentences in order.

❶ The children rescued Hugo.

❷ The children went to the ice cream shop.

❸ The children rescued Poppy.

❹ The children took Betty and Bob home.

________ → ________ → ________ → ________

Let's Review the Story

Fill in the blanks to review the story.

Problem	→	Solution

Problem

- Cody needed a job to save money to buy a new bike.
- The pet owners did not like him charging people to play with Jojo and Rex.

Solution

- He decided to start a __________ business.
- Cody gave the __________ back to his friends and let them play with the pets for free.

Problem

- Cody needed to learn how bank accounts pay interest.

Solution

- Cody went to the __________ and talked to a bank teller. She told him how __________ is paid and which __________ pay the most.

Problem

- Cody had too many pet sitting jobs and not enough time to take care of all of the animals.

Solution

- He hung "__________ Wanted" signs and hired __________ employees.

Problem

- Poppy the parrot got out of her cage.
- Hugo got out of his cage when Hanna left the door open.
- Cody was worried about how he would keep up with all of the pet sitting work once school started.

Solution

- Cody had David put bowls of birdseed out in the __________. Cody got Poppy on his __________ and put her in her cage.
- Cody found him huddled behind a glass __________ in the kitchen __________. Cody put Hugo back in his cage.
- Cody needed to __________ even more employees.

Let's Think & Talk

Think about the following questions and answer them freely.

❶ Have you ever worked for your pocket money? If you have, tell us what kind of work you did.

❷ Are you saving your pocket money to buy something? Tell us what it is.

❸ Have you ever been to a bank? Do you have a bank account? Go to the bank to find out how to get a bank account and explain it in detail.

❹ Tell us what kind of work you can do with your friends to make money like the work Cody did.

Let's Review the Story

Problem	→	Solution

Problem

- Cody needed a job to save money to buy a new bike.
- The pet owners did not like him charging people to play with Jojo and Rex.

Solution

- He decided to start a **pet sitting** business.
- Cody gave the **money** back to his friends and let them play with the pets for free.

Problem

- Cody needed to learn how bank accounts pay interest.

Solution

- Cody went to the **bank** and talked to a bank teller. She told him how **interest** is paid and which **accounts** pay the most.

Problem

- Cody had too many pet sitting jobs and not enough time to take care of all of the animals.

Solution

- He hung " **Help** Wanted" signs and hired **two** employees.

Problem

- Poppy the parrot got out of her cage.
- Hugo got out of his cage when Hanna left the door open.
- Cody was worried about how he would keep up with all of the pet sitting work once school started.

Solution

- Cody had David put bowls of birdseed out in the **yard**. Cody got Poppy on his **hand** and put her in her cage.
- Cody found him huddled behind a glass **vase** in the kitchen **cabinet**. Cody put Hugo back in his cage.
- Cody needed to **hire** even more employees.

After-reading Test

- Adventures in Pet Sitting
- Level 3
- 27 Questions

  (Vocabulary 7 / Reading Comprehension 16 /

  Sentence Structure & Grammar 4)

1. Which pair has the wrong past tense form of the listed verb?

① think — thought   ② bring — brought

③ feed — fed   ④ let — letted

2. Each word is a specific example of the word listed on the right side. Which one is an incorrect example?

① couch → furniture

② client → people

③ ferret → animal

④ hair salon → vehicle

※ Choose the right word for each blank. (3~4)

3. We won't have time to take care ______________ all of the pets.

① on   ② of

③ to   ④ in

4. From now on, I'll let people ride my scooter ____________ free.

① to   ② at

③ for   ④ into

※ Choose the word that has the given meaning. (5~6)

5. a loud, harsh cry that birds make

① squawk   ② groan

③ meow   ④ hop

6.

① sawdust   ② birdseed
③ perch   ④ whisker

7. What does the sentence mean in the story?

① Cody felt happy.
② Cody was disappointed.
③ Cody had a heart problem.
④ Cody dropped his heart-shaped money jar on the floor.

8. What did the dogs do when Cody tied their leashes to his handlebars?
① They pulled the scooter.
② They laid down to wait for his command.
③ They tried to get away.
④ They chewed on the leashes.

9. Why did Hanna and David want to ride on Cody's scooter?
① He had a fast scooter.
② They didn't have a fast scooter.
③ It looked like fun with the dogs.
④ They were very tired.

10. Who called Cody's father?
① Josh's brother
② Hanna's mother
③ David's father
④ the two dog owners

11. How can you know Jojo and Rex are NOT small dogs?

① They can jump high.

② They eat big bowls of food.

③ They can pull Cody's scooter and his friends.

④ They bark loudly.

12. Choose all of the things Cody did to take care of the animals.

① He combed the cat's fur.

② He walked the dogs.

③ He washed them every week.

④ He cleaned the animals' cages.

13. What did Mr. Beamer do when Cody told him how to save the money for his bike?

① He said the bike had already been sold.

② He shook Cody's hand and congratulated him.

③ He told Cody that the price was too expensive.

④ He gave Cody a high-five and patted him on the shoulder.

14. What money did Cody use to open his bank account?

① the money he received from his friends

② the money he saved due to his cash discount

③ the money he saved from mowing lawns

④ the money he received for his birthday

15. Why did Cody want to buy a new computer for his family?

① Their computer was broken.

② Their computer had a virus.

③ They did not have a computer.

④ Their computer was old.

16. How did Cody solve the problem of having so many animals to take care of?

① He worked long hours.

② He put up "Help Wanted" signs.

③ He told his friend he was sorry.

④ He closed his business.

17. How did Hugo escape?

① Hanna forgot to close the gate on his cage.

② Hugo squeezed between the bars of his cage.

③ Hugo used his teeth to open the cage door.

④ Hugo chewed through the side of his cage.

18. What did Cody think might happen to Hugo if they did NOT find him?

① Mrs. Taylor's cat might eat him.

② Mr. King's bird might grab him.

③ Betty and Bob might chase him.

④ He might get lost in the backyard.

19. What might happen to Poppy if they did NOT get her back in the house?

① She might get thirsty.

② She might get hungry.

③ She might fly away.

④ She might move in with some new people.

20. What did Cody tell Hanna hamsters like to do?

① play games

② nibble on corn

③ climb tall trees

④ hide in small spaces

21. How did Cody know to look in the cabinet under the sink?

    ① He heard Hugo scratching.

    ② Socks was watching the cabinet.

    ③ Hanna told him she had not looked there yet.

    ④ David told him to look there.

22. What is one reason Cody felt proud?

    ① He started a business and helped his friends get jobs.

    ② He knew he would do well in school.

    ③ He helped his parents at home.

    ④ He made a new friend.

23. What will Cody need to do when school starts?

    ① hire more children

    ② ride on the bus

    ③ give a gift to his teacher

    ④ eat breakfast every day

※ Choose the wrong part of each sentence. (24~25)

24.
I think I know where is Hugo.
   ①   ②   ③   ④

25.
She had a fluffy cat who would love to eat Hugo.
   ①   ②   ③   ④

※ Choose the correct order of the given words to complete each sentence. (26~27)

26.
He held out a finger _____(her, climb, to, for)_____ onto.

① to her climb for   ② for her to climb
③ for her climb to   ④ to climb for her

27.
I _____(give, going, to, am)_____ you a cash discount of 10%.

① give to am going   ② give going to am
③ am going to give   ④ am going give to

Memo

Memo

Memo

Memo

Suzanne Pitner

Suzanne Pitner is a teacher and writer who has enjoyed visiting Alaska, exploring Rome, teaching in China, and is looking forward to more world travel. She has a Master's Degree in Education, and is a graduate of the Long Ridge Writer's Group. In addition to writing educational articles and books, she writes historical fiction and contemporary fiction for young adults using the pen name Suzanne Lilly.

Adventures in Pet Sitting

Written by Suzanne Pitner
Illustrated by Inlae Cho

First Published in December 2014

Editorial Manager: Juyon Choi
Editors: Kyunghee Jang, Jiyeong Park
Designers: Eunhee Lee, Elim
Cover Designer: Eunhee Lee

Published and distributed by

Darakwon Bldg., 64-1 Jandari-ro, Mapo-gu, Seoul, Korea 121-894
Tel: 82-2-736-2031(ext. 250)   Fax: 82-2-736-2037
Homepage: www.ihappyhouse.co.kr
Publisher: Kyudo Chung

ISBN: 978-89-6653-163-9 18740 / 978-89-6653-156-1 18740(set)

[Components]
• 1 Audio CD (Recording Studio: Aram)
• Answer Keys & Korean Translation: Free download at www.ihappyhouse.co.kr